Theory Workbook

Grade **6**

Written by
Anna Butterworth, Anthony Crossland
Terence Greaves & Michael Jacques

ABRSM

First published in 1999 by ABRSM (Publishing) Ltd,
a wholly owned subsidiary of ABRSM, 4 London Wall Place, London EC2Y 5AU.

P14554

© 1999 by The Associated Board of the Royal Schools of Music

AB 2716

Extracts from the following copyright works are reproduced with permission:

Finzi, *Five Bagatelles* for clarinet and piano.
Kodály, *Te Deum*.
Hindemith, *Concerto for Orchestra*.
Set by Musonix

Printed in Great Britain by Caligraving Ltd, Thetford, Norfolk,
on materials from sustainable sources

Contents

The system of chord labelling used in this workbook is 'extended Roman'. It best identifies the sound quality of the chord and its function within the key. Please note, however, that examination candidates may use any recognised method of chord labelling, provided it presents a clear indication or a precise description of the harmony.

Introduction

This *Theory Workbook* provides straightforward information and advice about, and practice for, the Associated Board's Grade 6 theory exam papers. It focuses on the skills, knowledge and understanding that are being tested at the grade, exploring each specific element of the syllabus in some detail and providing insights into how candidates can approach their papers in a positive frame of mind and with every chance of success.

The workbook is complementary to the Board's range of related theory publications, in particular *The AB Guide to Music Theory* and *Harmony in Practice*. With all these, students will be supremely well-equipped to acquire the essential theory skills and understanding they need for their musical development in general and undertaking their Associated Board Grade 6 Theory exam in particular.

Philip Mundey
Director of Examinations

Question 1 (a)

In this question you will be asked to harmonise a short melody, indicating the chords in one of various ways. The melody will be about eight bars long in a major or minor key which is unlikely to exceed four sharps or four flats, and will be in a simple tonal style, such as a hymn or folk tune. Asterisks beneath the stave indicate the changes of chord and you have to decide which chords to use to obtain a convincing and musical harmonic flow. Remember that an asterisk may imply a change of chord *position* rather than an actual change of chord. A line after an asterisk means that the chord continues to apply.

The chords with which you are expected to be familiar are listed here and in the syllabus for Grade 6. (Note that there is a distinction between chords which you are expected to be able to use and those which you need only recognise.) You may, of course, use chords which are not listed, so long as you are familiar with them and can employ them to good musical effect.

Although you can use appropriate $\frac{5}{3}$, $\frac{6}{3}$ and $\frac{6}{4}$ chords on any degree of the major or minor scale, a satisfactory harmonisation may be possible using a limited number of chords and inversions. For example, a progression like I–iib–V–I is perfectly acceptable.

The melody chosen will not contain accidentals implying a modulation, which would force you to demonstrate that you can use chords to change key. However, the melody may be constructed so that it is possible to change key, and of course you may do so if you wish.

An awareness of stylistic features is useful, though it is not being tested as such in this question. A folk-like melody, for example, will probably require only a simple harmonic scheme, whilst a more hymn-like tune may require more chords to be used. However, the question primarily tests an ability to choose suitable chords to harmonise a melody, and matters of style are very much secondary to this.

You have some choice in how you answer the question. The introduction to the question in the exam paper is worded like this:

Indicate ONE chord at each of the places marked * to accompany the following melody. You may do so by writing roman numerals or any other recognised method of notation between the staves, OR by writing notes on the staves which provide a proper harmonic structure; but use only ONE of these methods.

This implies two main methods of approaching the question:

Method 1   The harmony may be indicated by roman numerals or chord symbols placed between the staves.

Method 2   The harmony may be shown by indicating notes on the staves.

Remember that you may use only **one** of these methods when answering the question in the exam.

Grade 6 chords

The harmonic vocabulary expected will include: the use of $\frac{5}{3}$, $\frac{6}{3}$ and $\frac{6}{4}$ chords on any degree of the major or minor (harmonic and melodic) scale; the recognition of the dominant seventh chord in root position, first, second and third inversions, and the supertonic seventh chord in root position and first inversion, in any major or minor key; and the figuring for all these chords.

Indicating the chords

In the working of the questions which follow, the system of chord indication known as **extended Roman**, which accurately describes the 'sound' of the chords, has been used. Two further methods, **basic Roman** and **figured Roman**, are also acceptable, as is the use of **jazz notation**. You will find useful information about these various systems in *Harmony in Practice*, Chord Labelling and *The AB Guide to Music Theory*, Part I 8/1–3 and Part II, Appendix D.

Whichever system you adopt, you must ensure that it presents a clear indication of the intended harmony.

Sample Question

Let us now work a sample question using each of the methods described on page 1.

WORKING THE QUESTION

Method 1

1. Decide on the **key** of the melody and write this in at the beginning of the stave.

2. Write out and **label the triads** in the key.

3. **Hum** through the melody (or, in the exam, sing it through in your head). It does not matter if you cannot find the exact pitch; choose a comfortable starting note, or, as this is practice work, use a keyboard or instrument to help you. Take time to get the intervals and rhythms right before you think about the chords.

4. **Mark in the main cadence points** and name the cadences. Here, these come at the fourth and eighth bars, but a subsidiary cadence may also occur in the second bar – you should look out for implied subsidiary cadences in an exam question, especially if the tempo is on the slow side. You may also find it helpful to add some phrasing to remind yourself where the phrase endings and cadence points come.

5. If you think the melody modulates and you have studied **modulation**, make a note of the related keys and bracket the modulation. Modulation is possible at the fourth bar particularly; however it is not in the syllabus for this question at Grade 6, so you will not be penalised if you do not change key.

It is very important not to miss out any of these steps. Aim to familiarise yourself thoroughly with the complete melody, rather than launching straight into writing chords from bar 1.

Your working so far should look like this:

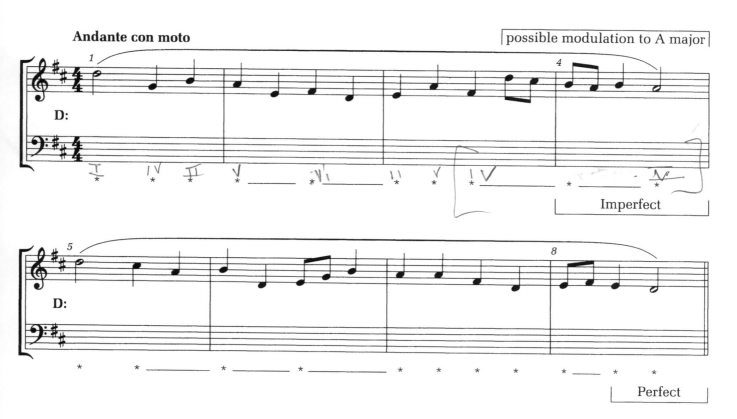

Look carefully through this skeleton working, first at the beginning and then at the two main cadence points. The first chord of bar 1 should firmly establish the tonic key with a root position chord of D major. Bar 4 could be either a perfect cadence in A major, if you wish to use a modulation, or an imperfect cadence in D major. It would also be possible to have a plagal cadence (IV–I) in D major here, but a definite cadence ending on the tonic both at the halfway point and the end of the melody would weaken the overall harmonic structure and is better avoided. Bar 8 will be a perfect cadence in D major.

Now look at the asterisks. These tell you where the chords are to go, but remember two vital points:

- They may denote *either* a change of chord *or* a change in the position of the previous chord.

- A horizontal line following an asterisk means that the chord continues without any change.

With these points in mind, look again at the three bars which have just been considered and the following should be clear:

Bar 1 The first asterisk requires a root position chord of D major. The next two asterisks could mean two positions of another chord or two separate chords.

Bar 4 The two halves of the bar require just one chord each, either V–I in A major if you are modulating, or ii–V or IV–V if an imperfect cadence in D major is chosen. If you choose to modulate, you should identify the new key to make the chord notation clear, as in the example below.

Bar 8 One chord is needed for the first two quavers, followed either by a different inversion of that chord or by a different chord. The last note will be harmonised by a root position chord of D major.

These chords and cadence points should now be labelled and will look something like this:

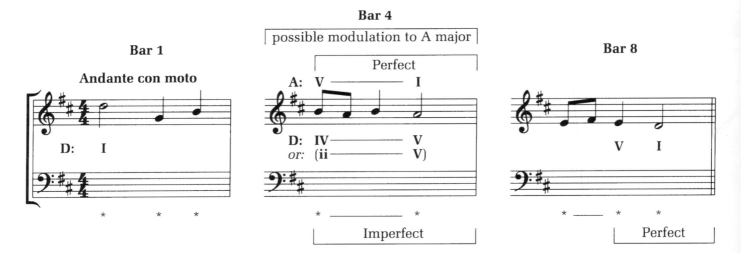

1. Hum through the melody again and work out a possible **harmonic rhythm**. This should help you decide which asterisks mean a change of chord and which mean a change of chord *position*. Bars 2, 4, 5 and 6 give a clue in that they clearly have just two changes of harmony per bar, and this would be a satisfactory pattern for the whole melody. Another point to remember, however, is that more frequent changes of harmony at the approach to cadences are common and give greater strength to the movement: for example, in bar 8, two different chords for the first half of the bar would be better than two positions of chord V.

2. Now you need to decide on the remainder of the chords and label them. Look at the notes of the melody line, and consulting your chart of triads in the key, identify the triad(s) to which each belongs and make a note of this. Some chords will be easy to choose: for example bar 2, where the first chord must be V. In other places more options are available, some of them of equal musical suitability, others less so, and it is vitally important that you play over (or if you are not a keyboard player, get a friend to play over) the various possibilities and so gain the ability to hear in your mind what you are writing.

The following points may also help to guide your choice of chords:

•   Bear in mind strong progressions such as the **progression of fifths**, i.e. I–IV–vii°–iii–vi–ii–V–I in a major key (see also *Harmony in Practice*, Chapter 9). It is often easier to work backwards from the cadence, for example, by asking 'What is the strongest chord before chord V which fits the melody note?' Your answer may well be, 'Chord iib', and this would be an excellent choice for the first beat of bar 8 as iib–V is a frequently heard cadence progression. ii–V is also common.

- Though you have only labelled the chords, remember that bass notes are implied by what you have written and the use of chord inversions will help greatly to achieve a less angular and more shapely bass line.

- Contrary motion between the bass and melody lines is always strong and should be freely used or implied.

Here is a completed working (with some alternative chord choices) which provides a satisfactory answer to the question:

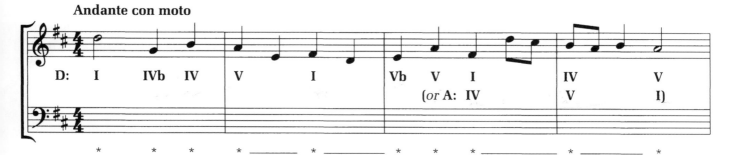

Remember; as bass notes are implied by your choice of chords, you must check carefully to ensure that no consecutive (parallel) fifths or octaves exist between the melody and the bass. For example, in the second half of bar 1, IV–IVb would give a satisfactory harmonic progression but would create consecutive octaves between the melody and bass line.

Method 2

In this option the question is completed by indicating notes on the staves, and three choices are open to you:

Choice 1   The use of a bass line and one inner part to complete the harmony.

Choice 2   The use of four-part harmony in vocal (SATB) style.

Choice 3   The use of a simple keyboard style.

 It must be emphasised that all the choices within Method 2 are more difficult than completing the question using Method 1. They do not attract any additional marks in the exam and it is recommended that you use Method 2 only if you are experienced in the techniques and confident working with them.

We will now look at ways of completing the question using each of these three choices.

Choice 1

This is the simplest option available in Method 2. It consists of working out the bass line and writing it on the stave, then adding an inner part to complete the harmony.

Up to the point where you have inserted chord labels, the steps to be followed are the same as those for Method 1. Here is a summary:

1. Familiarise yourself with the melody and its general style and character. Decide on the key, cadences, phrasing and any possible modulation.

2. Drawing from the complete set of chords for the key, label the chords as directed by the asterisks. (Chord labels for Method 2 should go below the staves as you will need the space between the staves for the inner part(s).) Put in the cadences first and then build up the remainder of the harmony. (Don't forget that working backwards from the cadence chords can be very helpful.)

Now add the bass line (stems go down for Choices 1 and 2), checking carefully for consecutives. The result should look something like this:

You are now ready to complete the harmony with an inner part.

Here (p.7) is a completed three-part version. Note that consecutive fifths and octaves must be avoided in all the parts and that the harmony should be as complete as possible. The root may be doubled unless it is the leading note, and the fifth omitted but the third of the chord should never be left out. In your final answer, chord labels should be erased or bracketed.

Andante con moto

Choice 2

In this option the question is completed by writing in four-part (SATB) style.

The initial steps are again the same as in Method 1, until you have labelled the chords.

Now add the bass line, checking carefully for consecutives, and then the inside parts (alto and tenor). Here, as when labelling the chords, you may find it preferable to complete the cadence bars first, then the opening, and finally the remaining inner parts.

> ▶ *The following basic rules of good four-part harmony writing should be noted* (see also *Harmony in Practice*, Chapters 3 and 4):
>
> * Normally the root of the chord is doubled.
>
> * Chord vii° (and chords ii° and vi° in a minor key) frequently sound poor in root position and should generally be used in first inversion.
>
> * At this stage it is better not to overlap the parts.
>
> * All voices should move melodically. This requires particular care, when working in a minor key, to avoid augmented and diminished melodic intervals, especially when the sharpened leading note is involved.
>
> * Consecutive fifths and octaves are not allowed. They are considered a serious breach of musical grammar because they dilute harmonic progressions by giving the effect of unison movement (in the case of consecutive octaves), or creating a bare, open sound which is very similar to the unison (in the case of consecutive fifths). Because of this, composers rarely used them until more recently, when they were employed for specific musical effect, but for exam purposes (i.e. when working with tonal harmony) they must be avoided.
>
> * The inside parts may be decorated with passing notes but make sure they do not give rise to consecutives.

The following shows the question completed by this method, Choice 2. Chord labels, introduced in the course of your working, should be erased or bracketed in your final answer.

Choice 3

In this choice a simple keyboard style is used, with two or three parts in the treble stave (R.H.) and one part in the bass (L.H.).

The steps for completing the question by Choice 1 should be followed until you reach the point of adding the inner part. You should then consult the text for Question 2 ('Realisation for the keyboard', p.27) and follow the recommendations which are given there.

Here is a good working for the keyboard:

The various options set out under Methods 1 and 2 represent the recommended ways of working Question 1(a). Note that the use of a bass line only in Method 2 is **not acceptable**, as this does not make the harmonic implications clear. The use of a **figured bass**, whilst possible as a recognised form of notation, is not generally recommended as it forms the alternative option, Question 1(b).

A good way of preparing generally for this question is to study simple harmonisations of folk tunes, hymns and so on, by playing them on a keyboard (or listening to recordings/asking someone to play to you if you do not play a keyboard instrument) while following the bass line and chord progressions being used in the music. This will help to develop your aural awareness and assist you to decide upon the best harmonic progressions to use. (Further useful information can be found in *Harmony in Practice*, Chapter 5.)

Question 1(a)   Sample Questions

Indicate ONE chord at each of the places marked * to accompany the following melodies. You may do so by writing roman numerals or any other recognised method of notation between the staves, OR by writing notes on the staves which provide a proper harmonic structure; but use only ONE of these methods.

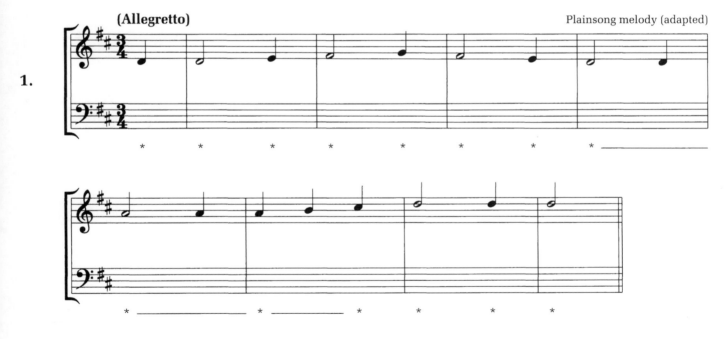

Allegro

Samuel Webbe: part song

3.

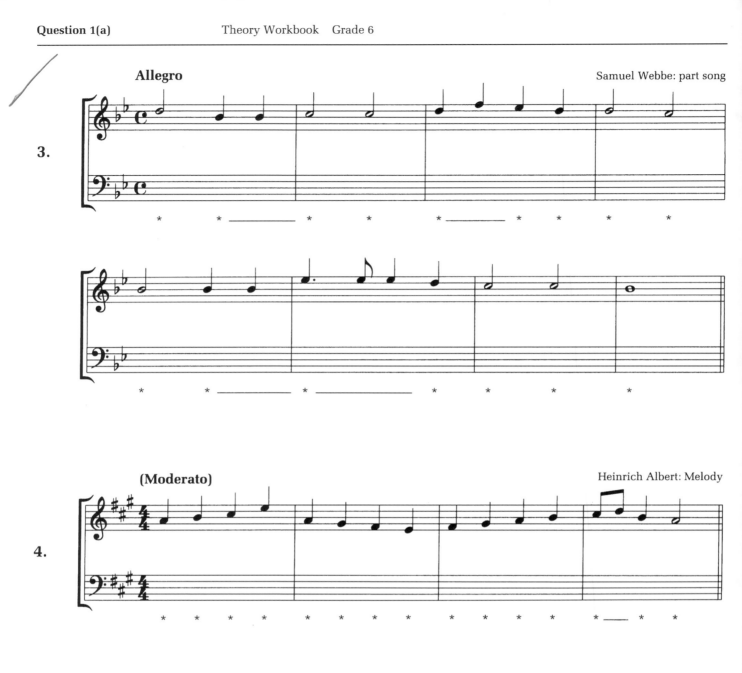

(Moderato)

Heinrich Albert: Melody

4.

(Slowly)

Traditional English melody (adapted)

5.

6.

(Moderato)   Austrian folk song (adapted)

7.

Allegro maestoso   Holst: 'Jupiter', from *The Planets* †

† Note that the implied harmony differs from the original.

8.

Moderato   Scheidt: 'Wehe Windgen, wehe' (adapted)

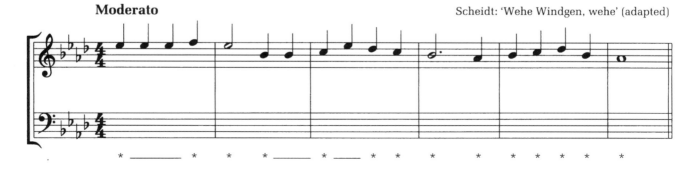

12.

13.

14.

Question **1 (b)**

In this alternative to Question 1(a) you will be asked to complete the bass line of a short melody and add suitable figures to indicate the harmony. The melody will be about eight bars long in a major or minor key which is unlikely to exceed four sharps or four flats, and will be simple in style. Asterisks beneath the bass stave indicate where the figures are to go and you have to decide which chords to use to obtain a convincing musical flow which maintains the style of the opening. As in Question 1(a) the asterisks may imply a change of chord position rather than an actual change of chord, and a line after an asterisk means that the chord continues to apply.

Although asterisks are used to indicate all chords and chord changes it is not necessary for you to figure $\frac{5}{3}$ chords, except when part of a $\frac{6}{4}$ $\frac{5}{3}$ cadential progression or if the fifth or third is altered chromatically.

Sample Question

We will now look at an exam-style question and go through the various steps necessary to complete it. Much of the procedure is similar to that for Question 1(a). You are urged to play through (or ask a friend to play through) all the harmonic options when working this question to teach your ear to discriminate between good and unsatisfactory progressions. The passage of music used here has been slightly adapted from a Flute Sonata by Loeillet.

Complete the bass line and add suitable figures as necessary, *from the last beat of bar 3*, at the places marked * in this passage. If you wish to use a $\frac{5}{3}$ chord leave the space under the asterisk blank, but $\frac{5}{3}$ chords must be shown as part of a $\frac{6}{4}$ $\frac{5}{3}$ progression or when chromatic alteration is required.

14

WORKING THE QUESTION

1. Decide on the key of the melody and mark it at the beginning of the stave.

2. Hum through the melody to fix its shape firmly in your mind. (Notice that the second phrase has been extended by sequence with the result that the passage is nine rather than eight bars long.)

3. Write out and label the triads in the key. Remember, as this is in a minor key:

   (a) the triads other than the tonic will have two alternatives because of the different forms of the 6th and 7th degrees of harmonic and melodic minor scales. (See also *Harmony in Practice*, Chapter 1.)

   (b) the first triad on the supertonic, ii°, and the second triads on the submediant and leading note, #vi° and #vii°, are diminished. The sound of the diminished 5th between the outer notes of the triad is somewhat harsh, and for this reason it is better to use these chords in first inversion, when the interval between the outer notes becomes a major 6th and is much more acceptable to the ear.

4. Mark in the cadence points, naming the cadences involved. These come at the fourth and ninth bars.

5. Modulation might be possible; make a note of it at this stage. Remember, however, that it is not expected of you in this question and you will not lose any marks if you do not use it.

6. Label the initial harmony in between the staves. In this style, the rate of harmonic change may be slower than in a hymn/chorale-type question.

Here is how the working should look at this stage:

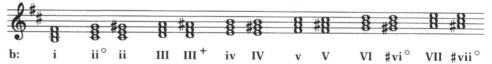

Bar 1   It should be clear that the first bar implies straightforward B minor tonic harmony (i), whilst

Bar 2   has dominant harmony in first inversion (Vb) followed by root position on the last beat (V).

Bar 3   begins with B minor again (i) which brings us almost to the cadence at bar 4.

Bar 4   is undoubtedly F♯ major – the dominant of B minor (V) – but the approach chord on the last beat of bar 3 offers the following possibilities:

(a) Maintaining the B minor harmony with a first inversion chord (ib), and regarding the C♯ in the melody as an accented passing note,

(b) Chromatically altering chord ii to include E♯ as well as G♯, which would imply a modulation to F♯ major, or

(c) Using chord ii°b to give a normal ii°b–V imperfect cadence (regarding the B in the melody as a passing note).

The first option **(a)** creates a nice dissonance but rather unrelieved tonic (i) and dominant (V) harmony. The second option **(b)** is possible, since the F♯ major chord leads naturally into the B minor harmony of bar 5. The third option **(c)** is the most likely solution using a simple imperfect cadence.

Bar 5   is clearly B minor harmony (i) but the asterisks give us the possibility of some variety by alternating between first inversion and root position.

Bars 8–9   the final cadence point. The cadential $\frac{6}{4}$ (ic–V–i) progression is appropriate here. Notice the acceleration of the harmonic rhythm at the approach to the cadence.

We will now add these details to the working:

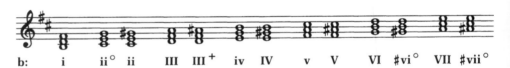

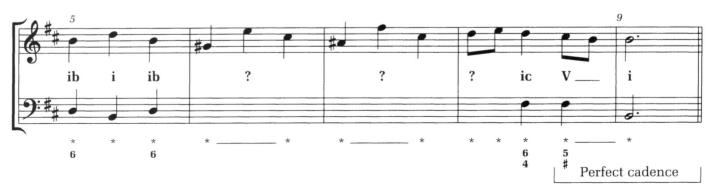

It now remains to complete bars 6, 7 and the first part of bar 8.

Bar 6 If you look at the chart of triads you will see that the second supertonic triad (ii) is a possibility for the whole bar, since it contains all the melody notes. However the use of iia at the beginning of the bar causes parallel movement to a fifth from the previous treble and bass notes and sounds ugly, whilst the use of iib–iia in bar 6 will cause consecutive octaves. Another look at the triad chart shows that the second subdominant triad (IV) could be used for the first two beats. This sounds good, and the supertonic chord will follow smoothly on the third beat, though it must be used in first inversion to avoid consecutive octaves with the melody.

Bar 7 The asterisks indicate the same harmonic rhythm as bar 6, underlying the sequential nature of the passage. For the first two beats experiment will quickly show that, of the two chord possibilities (III⁺ or V), the augmented mediant chord gives an unsatisfactory sound and that dominant harmony works best for the whole bar. The first chord must be root position; a first inversion would not only double the melody's A♯ leading note but would also result in an awkward E–A♯ melodic interval with the preceding bass note. This means Vb for the third beat of the bar.

Bar 8 Two chords are required here for the first beat. The first of these is dictated by the last bass note of bar 7, an A♯ leading note which needs to resolve onto a tonic B, giving a chord of B minor in root position. For the second quaver two choices are possible, iv or ii°b, and either of these would provide a satisfactory link with the following $^6_4$ chord.

In all of the above procedures the importance of hearing the various alternatives, either by playing the chords yourself or asking someone to play them for you, must again be stressed.

Here is the completed working. Chord labels have been left in (bracketed) for reference:

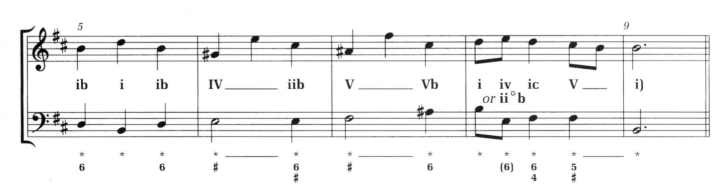

Now look carefully through the working to ensure that no consecutive octaves or fifths have slipped in.

Next, check that all the figuring is correct.

> *Here is a reminder of the main rules* (see also *Harmony in Practice*, Chord Labelling and *The AB Guide to Music Theory*, Part I 8/4):
>
> - No figure means a $\frac{5}{3}$ chord.
>
> - A first inversion, $\frac{6}{3}$, chord is indicated by the single figure 6. Be sure not to confuse this with a $\frac{6}{4}$ chord. (You will find some information about the use and resolution of the $\frac{6}{4}$ chord under Question 2 (see p.26).)
>
> - All accidentals contained in the melody line or implied by the figuring must be shown.
>
> - An accidental on its own beneath the stave refers to the note a third above the bass. Thus the third of the last chord in bar 2 will be sharpened (A♯) and the last chord of bar 6 will be a first inversion chord containing a G♯.

Once you are satisfied with your working you can look through the piece and see if you wish to decorate the bass line in any way. It is not essential to do this and over-decoration can do more harm than good, but there may be an opportunity for a little embellishment, especially at any point where the bass is static, for instance in bar 4 of our worked example (p.17). In the original composition, Loeillet decorates this bar with quaver movement, as is shown below.

If you do introduce any decoration be very sure that it does not cause consecutives or alter the harmony required by the asterisks, and do not, of course, make any alterations to the given part of the question.

Finally, as this piece is in a minor key, you have the option of ending with a **tierce de Picardie** (the tonic major chord ending a minor-key passage of music). Since tonic minor harmony occurs in a number of bars in this passage, particularly in the penultimate bar, a tierce de Picardie would give welcome variety and surprise at the end, and is a feature of Baroque style.

Question 1(b)   Sample Questions

Complete the bass lines and add suitable figures as necessary at the places marked * in the following passages. If you wish to use a $\frac{5}{3}$ chord leave the space under the asterisk blank, but $\frac{5}{3}$ chords must be shown as part of a $\frac{6}{4}\frac{5}{3}$ progression or when chromatic alteration is required.

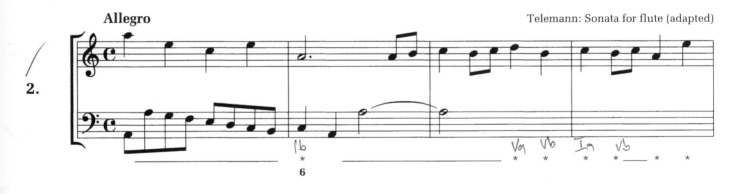

Tempo di minuetto

Telemann: Sonata for violin

Allegro

Fischer: Bourrée for harpsichord

Brightly   Old English melody (adapted)

5.

Allegro   Old English air (adapted)

6.

7.

8.

(Andante)   Philidor: Flute sonata

9.

```
*  ___  *  *  ___  *        ___       *  ___  *    *  _____
#  ___  6  6#  ___  6
```

```
*  _____  *  _____  *  _____  *  _____   *    *    *    *  _____   *  _____
```

Allegro   Handel: Gavotte for flute

10.

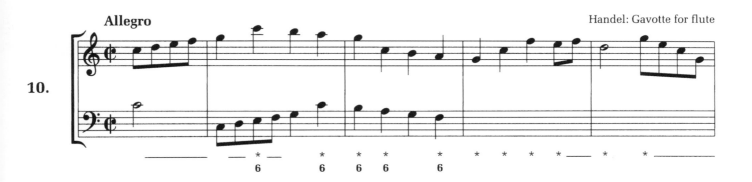

```
   _____   ___  *       *    *    *      *    *    *    *  ___  *     *  _____
              6          6    6    6      6
```

```
*  ___  *  ___  *  _____  *  ___  *  ___  *  ___  *  ___   *  ___  *  ___  *  _____  *
```

Question 2

This question presents you with a short extract of about four bars of figured bass and you will be asked to realise the chords, that is, to complete the harmony which they indicate, either by writing for four-part voices (SATB) or for keyboard. The extract will be in a major or minor key which is unlikely to exceed four sharps or four flats.

The bass figures will be limited to $^5_3$, $(^6_3)$ and $^6_4$, and if in a minor key, the question may include accidentals and altered chords, such as ii, IV or V, or the **tierce de Picardie**. Below is an example of chords altered in this way, with the changed notes in the melody which is part of the melodic minor scale (see also *Harmony in Practice*, Chapter 11). It is, of course, possible for altered notes to appear in any part. Remember that sharp, flat or natural signs under the stave which do not have a figure attached to them affect the note a **third** above the bass note. Thus the final chord is a tierce de Picardie, and the relevant B♮ has been inserted in brackets:

The harmony expected will be mostly note-against-note, though correctly used passing notes or other notes of decoration may be put in to add interest if you wish. Suspensions, however, will always be indicated in the figuring and should not be put in anywhere else.

The question will not require you to use modulation.

Sample Question

We will now look at a passage of figured bass, introduced as it is likely to appear in the exam, and suggest a method for providing an effective realisation.

Writing for four-part voices (SATB) or keyboard, realise this figured bass. Assume that all chords are $^5_3$ unless otherwise indicated.

WORKING THE QUESTION

1. Decide on the key of the passage and write it in at the beginning.

2. Hum through the bass line to familiarise yourself with it and especially with the final cadence.

3. On a piece of rough manuscript paper write out the bass line, with figures, and then mark, as dots, the notes forming the chords above each bass note, counting the intervals from the bass note. This will identify the chords for you. The result should be:

At this stage in your completion of the question it is important to have the following two points quite clear in your mind:

*   No figure beneath a bass note means a straightforward $\frac{5}{3}$, root position chord.

* $\frac{6}{3}$ or first inversion chords are used so frequently that they are usually indicated simply by '**6**'.

4. Invent a convincing **melody line**. The following points should help:

*   The notes of the melody will be selected from the chords which you have already sketched in.

*   Look for a line which has some shape and interest and which moves naturally towards the cadence. Most melody lines end on the tonic note at the cadence (perfect), preceded either by the leading note or the super-tonic.

*   Contrary motion between the melody and bass line is musically strong.

*   Avoid awkward leaps or diminished or augmented intervals in your melody line. On completion hum or play it through.

*   Check carefully for consecutives with the bass line.

Here is a satisfactory melodic line which has been worked out using these guidelines:

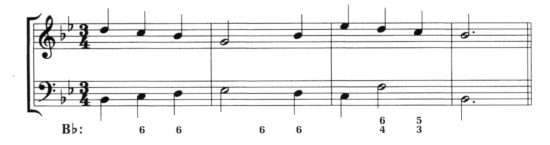

The final stage involves filling in the inner parts (alto and tenor), also using notes from the chords which have been sketched in. Before you do this, read the notes on the following page.

▶ *The following principles of good harmonic practice should be observed:*

- Normally the root of the chord is doubled. Be very careful not to confuse the *root* of the chord with the *bass note* of the chord. In $\frac{6}{3}$ chords the root will be the note a sixth above the bass and in $\frac{6}{4}$ chords it will be a fourth above the bass.

- It is better not to overlap the parts; the alto note of a chord should not be lower than the tenor note of the adjacent chords.

- A gap of more than one octave should occur only between the bass and tenor parts.

- Each part should stay comfortably within its range and ideally should have some melodic interest. Be careful to avoid awkward leaps and intervals, particularly if you are working in a minor key.

- Check carefully, as you go along, for consecutive fifths and octaves.

A special note about the $\frac{6}{4}$ chord (see also *Harmony in Practice*, Chapter 7.)

In this sample working you will have seen that a second inversion or $\frac{6}{4}$ chord is used in the final cadence. This is known as a **cadential $\frac{6}{4}$ chord**, Ic, and it normally moves to chord V thus:

- The note a sixth above the bass moves down to the fifth.

- The note a fourth above the bass moves down one step to the third.

- The bass note should be doubled in the $\frac{6}{4}$ chord and then repeated *in the same two parts* in the $\frac{5}{3}$ resolution chord.

- Sometimes the movement of the part-writing is clarified by the insertion of lines between the figures: $\frac{6}{4} - \frac{5}{3}$

✳ *Remember not to confuse $\frac{6}{4}$ figuring with '6', the $\frac{6}{3}$ or first inversion chord.*

Another version of the $\frac{6}{4}$ chord which may be encountered in this question is the **passing $\frac{6}{4}$**. Here the $\frac{6}{4}$ is used as an intermediate chord in the progression Ia to Ib or vice versa, or IVa to IVb or vice versa. In this case the best treatment is to make your top melody notes the same as the bass, but in reverse order. The following two examples should make the procedure clear and also show the best treatment for the inner parts:

Here (p.27) is a good completed working of the sample question. It should be noted that the parallel fifths between the alto and tenor parts in bar 1 are permissible, as the second chord is diminished.

Realisation for the keyboard

Instead of completing this question in the four-part vocal format, you have the option of working it for keyboard. This usually means the use of two or three notes in the top stave (R.H.) whilst the bottom stave (L.H.) should show the bass line only.

You should follow the procedure given for the four-part vocal version of this question, up to and including the writing of the melody line. You should then insert the inner part(s) on the right-hand stave.

Each right-hand chord should consist of two or three notes, but you should try to ensure that the right hand together with the bass line forms as complete a harmony as possible for each chord. Be particularly careful not to omit the third.

The right-hand notes should be grouped together as chords on one stem unless a part moves independently, in which case stem the chords according to their rhythmic values, as in the following example:

The usual prohibitions apply to consecutive fifths and octaves and you should check your working carefully for these. It is only too easy, in keyboard realisation, to produce block chordal movement which gives rise to faults such as the following (the consecutives have been illustrated):

Remember that you do not have to keep the rhythm the same in every part, and passing notes may be introduced if you wish, as long as your realisation follows the harmony indicated by the figures and does not break any grammatical rules.

Here is a good realisation of the sample question:

Question 2   Sample Questions

Writing for four-part voices (SATB) or keyboard, realise these figured basses.
Assume that all chords are $\frac{5}{3}$ unless otherwise indicated.

6.

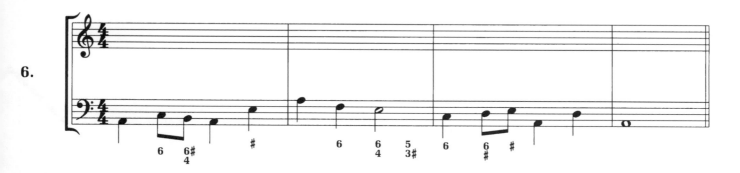

7.

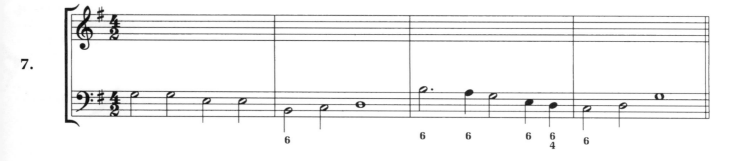

8.

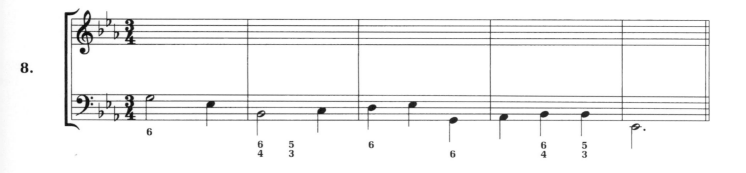

9.

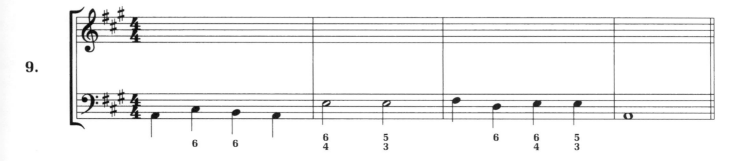

10.

Question 3(a)

In this question you will be given the opening of a melody and then asked to complete it, taking account of the instructions. The melody could be in any clef (though most likely in the treble or bass) and will be in a major or minor key which is unlikely to exceed four sharps or four flats. It will be firmly tonal in character and a simple, orthodox harmonic basis will be implied.

The question may indicate the style of the melody, for example by asking you to continue a march, a gigue or a lullaby. The melodic opening given will usually have a clearly defined key and character, and sometimes a composer's name will be shown. You should look out for any clues such as these and see that your answer is consistent with the type of melody implied.

The required length of the complete piece will be stated and will generally be between eight and ten bars. An eight-bar melody consisting of balanced two- or four-bar phrases is the most straightforward to construct, and this pattern has been followed in the sample working here. If you are more experienced at writing melodies you might wish to extend your working to nine or ten bars, possibly by the use of sequence, but this is by no means essential for a good working of this question.

It is quite likely that you will be asked to make a modulation to the dominant, the subdominant, or the relative major or relative minor, usually by the end of the melody. Appropriate performance directions will also be required, such as phrasing, articulation marks and dynamics. A limited number of instrument-specific instructions (such as pizz. or arco for string pieces) may also be suitable in some cases, but you are advised not to add these unless you are quite confident of being able to use them to good musical effect.

Either an instrument will be specified, or you will be given a choice. Bear in mind the following points:

- Try to imagine the sound of the instrument in your head and ensure that your melody is suitable to its character.

- On the whole it is better to avoid using notes at the extreme top or bottom of the instrument's range. If you do use these extremes you should be careful of dynamics, especially with woodwind and brass instruments. Remember, for example, that it is easier to play loudly rather than quietly on the lowest notes of the oboe or bassoon, whilst it is easier to play quietly rather than loudly at the bottom end of a flute. It is difficult to play quietly at the top end of a horn or trumpet.

- It may be possible to introduce some characteristic playing techniques of the instrument, such as double-stopping for strings, but these should be used only if you really understand them and can use them convincingly. Candidates sometimes use such devices quite inappropriately, and the safest rule is, if it isn't effective or necessary, don't use it.

- Remember that the primary requirement for this question is a shapely, well-structured melody, with straightforward dynamics, phrasing and articulation.

You may find it useful to refer to chapters 18–20 of *The AB Guide to Music Theory*, Part II, when considering aspects of melody and writing for string, woodwind and brass instruments.

Sample Question

Let us now look at an exam-style question and explore ways to complete it.

Continue this Lament for unaccompanied cello to form a piece of between eight and ten bars in length. End the piece with a modulation to the relative major and add performance directions as appropriate.

WORKING THE QUESTION

1. First establish the tonality in your mind. The required modulation to the relative major implies a minor key, and the one-sharp key signature and leading note D♯ in bar 2 confirm the key as E minor.

2. Sing the given opening in your head to establish its character and mood, noting the tempo indication and any dynamics and slurs/phrase marks. Try also to imagine the actual instrumental sound – in this case, a cello.

3. Fix in your mind the type of melody which is required, noting the clues of the word 'Lament' in the introduction to the question, the tempo marking of 'Andante' and the minor key. Obviously, some kind of sad, steadily flowing, song-like piece is intended.

4. Consider the overall range of your melody. Working on the basis of a total length of eight bars, the range should not be too narrow, and one suitable plan would be to introduce a fairly high climax point about three-quarters of the way through, giving the complete piece a good curving shape, building up to the climax and then down to the end.

5. Now sketch a plan of the complete melody by putting in the bar-lines, the given bars, the opening key and the modulation which is required at the end. The result should look like this:

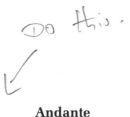

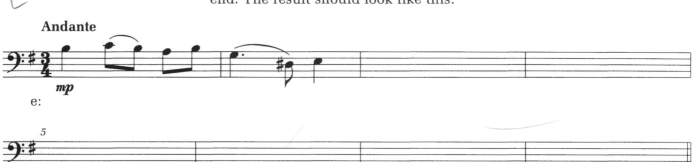

G major

6. Work out a proper harmonic foundation for the melody. The importance of this cannot be over-stressed; many students' workings fail because this aspect is neglected. Your melody should normally suggest to the ear a proper musical progression of chords which could be played under it.

With a melody of only eight bars the procedure is not as daunting as might be thought. You could fix two main cadences, with suitable approach chords, and a convincing move away from the first cadence.

Look again at the skeleton plan above. You have an opening fixed in E minor and your final modulation to G major is sketched in. This modulation would be best achieved by a perfect cadence in G major, and a good approach would be to use the supertonic chord, giving the progression ii–V–I in G major. These chords should be labelled under the stave.

The logical place for another definite cadence is at the halfway point, and here you could use an imperfect cadence. As you are still in the key of E minor this would mean a chord of B major at bar 4. This could be approached in various ways: in this case let us use the subdominant (in E minor), giving a iv–V progression. If these chords are sketched in, our skeleton working will look like this:

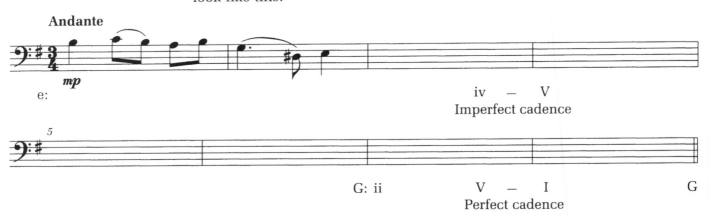

It now remains to complete the gaps in the harmonic structure of bars 3, 5 and 6. Bar 3 is simple, as the subdominant harmony may be implied throughout the bar. Bars 5 and 6 need a little more thought, as there are various options.

Let us consider bar 5 first. The preceding dominant chord of B major could lead us back to E minor, but having begun the piece with two bars of E minor harmony this course would be a little dull. A better move here would be to use C major harmony (VI in E minor), giving the impression of an interrupted cadence, and moving us neatly towards our destination key of G major. In the first part of bar 6 we could use D major (V in G major). This could be followed by G major, but it would be weak to anticipate the final cadence in this way. A much stronger solution would be to imply another interrupted cadence by using E minor harmony for the second half of bar 6. This would link very smoothly with the ii–V–I harmony of bars 7 and 8.

The complete harmonic skeleton would then appear like this:

The next stage is to create the melodic line itself.

It has already been pointed out that you should have a clear sense of the overall character and shape of the melody. You should now consider the following factors:

- The complete melody should show a properly balanced **phrase structure**. Usually an opening of two bars will be given, and this should be answered by another two-bar phrase. The second half should consist of either two two-bar phrases or a single four-bar phrase.

- To maintain a regular phrase structure, if the given opening begins on the first beat of the bar you must ensure that the subsequent phrases do the same. If the given opening begins with an **anacrusis** (that is, an upbeat), then the following phrases must do the same. Ends of phrases should be written to allow for this, using longer or shorter notes or rests if necessary so that the next phrase can begin on the correct beat of the bar.

     The following example of dealing with an anacrusic opening should make this clear:

- Melody notes approached or quitted by a leap should be derived from the chords suggested by your harmonic structure, except for inessential notes such as appoggiaturas.

- Melody notes approached or quitted by step may be passing notes (accented or unaccented), auxiliary notes or other notes of decoration, and you should be familiar with the correct use of all these.

- If you are writing for a wind instrument remember that you must allow the player to breathe! In a more slow-moving piece breaths can usually be taken between phrases. At faster tempi it will be necessary to insert rests.

- If you are writing for a string instrument and you would like the player to change from arco to pizz. or vice versa, remember that they will need time to do this.

- Your melodic structure should relate to, and grow out of, the given opening, but should not be merely a slavish copy of it. Examiners often see unsatisfactory workings such as the following:

You should look carefully at the given opening, particularly for any elements of it which might offer scope for development or variation. In our example, the four-quaver group of notes in the first bar and the rhythmic and melodic shape of the second bar offer possibilities. Remember that rhythmic aspects of the given opening are just as useful in developing your melody as pitch shapes.

The most successful melodic development usually comes from a careful combination of both aspects – melodic and rhythmic – and you should try to gain as much practice as you can – at first by writing answering two-bar phrases to given openings and then embarking on full eight- to ten-bar melodies. Remember, always work to a definite harmonic basis.

Here is a complete working of the sample melody in which the above principles have been applied:

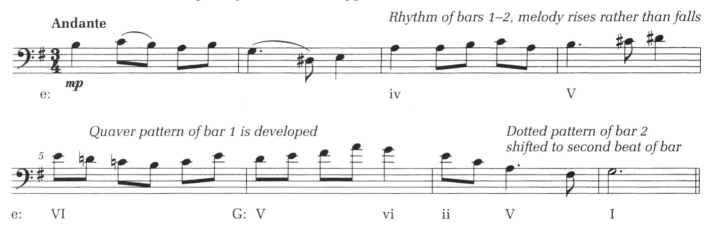

You will see that bars 3 and 4 are rhythmically the same as bars 1 and 2 and melodically an approximate inversion of them. The four-quaver rhythmic grouping appears also in bars 5 and 6, but some variety is achieved by using another pair of quavers in bar 5, and in bar 6 by moving the quaver figure to the first two beats of the bar. Bars 7–8 use the dotted rhythmic figure but here a shift away from the first two beats of the bar avoids monotony. The melodic shape has the desired curve, with a gradual rise in pitch to the climax point in bar 6 followed by a falling away to the end, and the harmonic structure has been adhered to.

All that now remains is to put in some expression marks and performance directions. See that these are always used to proper musical purpose and not merely to show off the extent of your knowledge of dynamic signs and Italian terms! In this particular melody, which is written for cello, it would also be appropriate to use the tenor clef for the higher notes, thus avoiding the necessity for numerous ledger lines.

The following is a final working of the question. The chord indications have been removed but you would not be penalised if you left them in your answer.

In equipping yourself properly to answer this question you should work out before the exam harmonic schemes for all the possible modulations. These modulations are:

(a) Major key, with modulation to dominant, subdominant or relative minor.

(b) Minor key, with modulation to dominant, subdominant or relative major.

This procedure may seem rather tedious and mechanical, but to have these relationships clear in your mind helps towards completing a satisfactory answer and also saves a considerable amount of time in the exam.

Question 3(a)   Sample Questions

Continue these openings to make melodies of between eight and ten bars in length. Write for the instruments indicated and include modulations as specified. Appropriate performance directions should be added.

1.   Minuet for violin, modulating at the end to the dominant.

2.   Siciliano for oboe, modulating at the end to the relative major.

3.   March for trombone, modulating at the end to the subdominant.

4.   Hornpipe for bassoon, modulating at the end to the dominant.

5.   Gavotte for violin, modulating at the end to the relative minor.

6.   Minuet for trumpet, modulating at the end to the dominant.

7.   Elegy for cello, modulating to the relative major but ending in the tonic.

8.   Sarabande for flute, modulating at the end to the dominant.

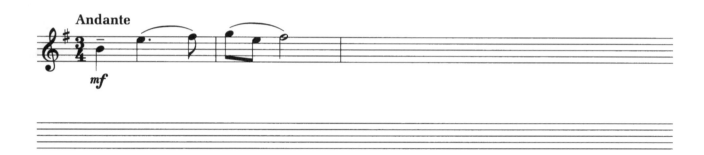

9.   Cradle Song for horn, modulating at the end to the relative minor.

10.   Air for clarinet, modulating at the end to the subdominant.

Question **3**(b)

This question is similar to Question 3(a), but the given opening will be in a freer style, perhaps modal in character (like a folk song), or with some particular rhythmic characteristic.

The melodic opening may be in any clef (though most likely in the treble or bass) and in a major or minor key (or mode) which is unlikely to exceed four sharps or four flats. The total number of bars required will be not less than eight. An instrument will be specified or a choice of instrument may be given and appropriate performance directions requested. You will not normally be required to make a modulation although you may if you wish to.

Much of the technique and most of the procedural steps for working this question are the same as for Question 3(a), so you should familiarise yourself thoroughly with them. Note particularly the need to produce a 'skeleton' of the given opening, to insert bar-lines for the complete melody, to mark the cadence points and the harmonic basis, to think in terms of balanced two- or four-bar phrases, and remember the various suggestions for obtaining good melodic shape and interest.

The main decision you will have to make is whether or not to introduce a modulation. It is perfectly possible, within the space of eight bars, to create a satisfactory melody which does not modulate, but special care must be taken to avoid too much repetition of melodic or rhythmic figures, which can be monotonous. There is no doubt that a well-thought-out and executed modulation is a good way of adding strength to a melody.

Let us now look at two sample workings. The first of these will have characteristic rhythmic features and no modulation; the second will be modal in character, with a modulation to the dominant, and will also start with an anacrusis. Though the intermediate steps in building up the answers have been omitted, it is essential that you go through them in the exam.

Both examples are introduced as they might appear in an exam paper.

Sample Question 1

Continue this opening for unaccompanied oboe to make a complete piece of not less than eight bars in length. You may make any modulation or modulations you wish, or none if you prefer. Add performance directions as appropriate.

WORKING THE QUESTION

The lively, energetic character of the melody is clearly indicated by the tempo
marking and by the number of leaps which occur in the opening. The main
rhythmic feature is the syncopation in bar 2, which gives the effect of 3/4
rather than 6/8 time, but the little rhythmic figure in the first half of bar 1 is
also significant. They will both be important in the completed sample working,
as follows:

The essential implied harmonic framework (see p.31, paragraph 6) was worked
out as follows:

The two rhythmic features mentioned above form the backbone for the whole
melody. The opening half-bar figure begins bar 3, but a tone higher, and the
syncopated figure of bar 2 recurs in bar 4, this time in inverted form in the
dominant key. This is not a modulation to the dominant but merely an implied
imperfect cadence, and the D♯ in bar 3 is a chromatic auxiliary note which is
then immediately naturalised. A new rhythm has been introduced for the
second half of bar 3 to prevent the second two bars from becoming too slavish
a copy of the first two.

The opening rhythmic figure begins bar 5 and ends bar 6 (slightly shortened
to allow the player to breathe) but, in between, the syncopated device is used
in a different way, creating two suspensions and giving the melody the form
of a rising sequence, shaping neatly upwards to the top B climax in bar 6. Bar
7 is virtually an inverted form of bar 1, and bar 8 combines the two rhythmic
features by throwing the final note unexpectedly onto the last quaver beat of
the first half-bar.

Sample Question 2

This sample question shows the completion of a modal, folk-like melody.

Continue this opening for unaccompanied flute to make a complete piece of not less than eight bars in length. You may make any modulation or modulations you wish, or none if you prefer. Add performance directions as appropriate.

WORKING THE QUESTION

Let us first consider the modal character of the melody. This derives from the key of G minor, but uses the flattened leading note (F♮ instead of F♯) as at the beginning, where dominant–tonic harmony is implied across the first bar line. We will decide on a broad harmonic scheme based on an implied modulation to the dominant key (D minor) at the half-way point, and back to G minor at the end. In reaching the dominant key at bar 4 we must ensure that the approach chord of A major (the dominant chord of the dominant key) also has a flattened third (the leading note of the new key) in order to maintain the style; it will therefore be a chord of A minor. The effect of the modulation will be reinforced by introducing an E♮ at some appropriate point.

The other characteristic feature of this example is the anacrusis. You will see that the melody begins on the fourth beat of the bar, so to maintain a regular phrase structure the subsequent phrases must begin in the same way.

A satisfactory completed working could look like this:

The significance of the E♮s in connection with the modulation should be clear, and brackets have been added to indicate the phrase structure and show how the anacrusis has been maintained. Though the second half is shown as one four-bar phrase, it is perfectly possible to punctuate the phrase before the last beat of bar 6 (indeed, a flute player, for example, might wish to take a slight breath at this point, hence the broken bracket).

Here, too, the melody has been constructed on a logically implied harmonic basis. The flowing, *cantabile* style of the melodic opening has been maintained and some melodic and rhythmic figures, such as the first half of bar 2, have been re-used in different contexts.

These, then, are two typical melodic types which might be used in Question 3(b). It should be apparent, however, that the two options available in Question 3 differ only slightly from each other and you may well not make a choice until you look at the exam paper and see which of the two melodic openings attracts you more.

Question 3(b)   Sample Questions

Continue the following openings for the instruments specified to make complete pieces of not less than eight bars in length. You may make any modulation or modulations you wish, or none if you prefer. Add performance directions as appropriate.

1.   Fanfare for trumpet.

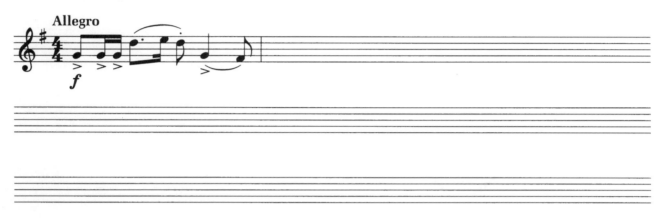

2.   Lullaby for flute.

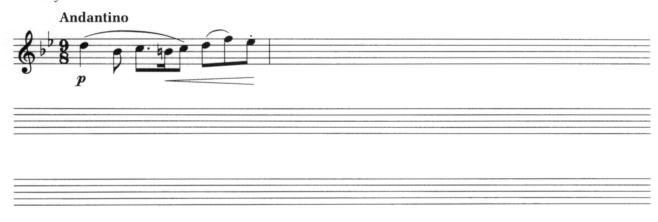

3.   Folk-like melody for cello.

4.   Air for flute.

5.   March for bassoon.

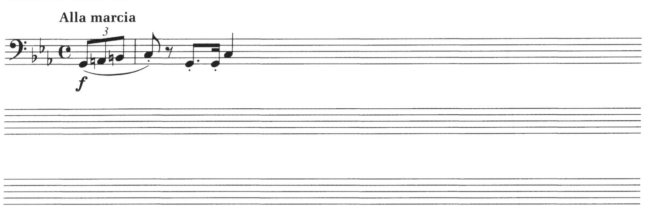

6.   Air for clarinet.

7.   Scherzo for cello.

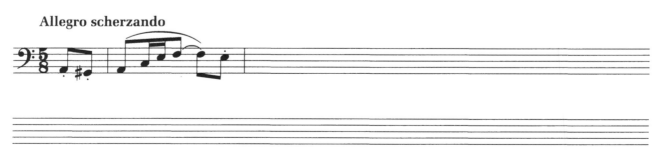

8.   Solemn melody for trombone.

9.   Sarabande for oboe.

10.   Lament for violin.

11.   Aria for horn.

Question 4

In this question you will be given an extract of music and will be asked a number of questions which test both your understanding of it and your ability to apply the theoretical knowledge you have acquired. The syllabus gives a wide range of possibilities for the choice of extracts, and past papers have used music written on systems of two or three staves, for example keyboard music or solo instrument (or voice) with piano, and occasionally music with systems of four staves. The music will be tonal in style.

Questions 4 and 5 together will attempt to cover as many aspects of the syllabus as possible in any one exam paper. **Occasionally, one slightly longer extract with questions worth a total of 50 marks may be used to cover the ground included in Questions 4 and 5.** An example of this is shown in the Specimen Paper for Grade 6. (Each theory paper is marked out of a total of 100.)

Following the requirements of the syllabus for Grade 6, questions will be asked on:

The key scheme

You may be asked to identify keys and modulations, cadences and harmonic sequences and you should note that the modulations are not restricted to those listed in the syllabus which relate to the melodic composition question.

Structure

You may be asked to show the main phrase structure of an extract either by describing it briefly, drawing square brackets over the staves to illustrate it or by completing statements about it. Structural devices such as ground bass, sequences, imitation, use of a motif, augmentation and diminution may well be included. Phrases may be compared so you can name the similarities and differences between them.

Harmony

This can be tested in various ways such as identification of the chords listed in the syllabus, either by being required to name specific chords which are numbered or marked with an asterisk, or by being required to find a named chord and specify its location in the extract. Root positions and the inversions listed in the syllabus may be tested, as well as the knowledge to describe them as major, minor, augmented or diminished and to state the prevailing key when it is not obvious or given. Pedal points on the tonic and dominant in particular (including those which are not in the bass) may also feature.

Aspects of melody

Under this topic you may be asked to identify imitation, melodic sequences, inversions, intervals (which may also be tested harmonically), and notes of melodic decoration such as passing, changing and auxiliary notes, acciaccaturas and appoggiaturas, as well as other notes which are not essential to the harmony. You may also be required to write out in full a bar or a passage marked with an ornament or an abbreviation sign as you think it should be played.

General

The paper may include a number of general questions asking you to describe or comment on certain features of the extract, such as aspects of rhythm, dynamics, word setting and the meaning of terms and symbols, including those from earlier grades. These features may also be tested by asking you to complete a series of statements or by asking you to indicate whether a statement is true or false. You might also be asked to suggest from a list the name of a likely composer of the extract, or a period during which it might have been composed, giving reasons for your choice.

Question 4   Sample Questions

Here are a number of exam-style practice tests. The first test shows the typical number of questions that would be asked in an exam, together with an example of how the marks might be distributed, adding up to the usual total of 25 for the whole exercise. In order to make full use of the other extracts, tests 2 to 6 contain more questions than you would be asked on a single exam paper. The marks for each individual section could well vary from paper to paper, according to the difficulty and time likely to be needed to complete that section.

The way the syllabus is covered should be evident from the variety in the presentation and wording of the questions.

As well as completing the following sample questions, you can ask yourself similar questions about pieces you are preparing for performance. In fact, some of the extracts in this workbook have been taken from pieces set for practical exams. Studying the theoretical background of a piece can enhance and enlighten a performance of it, and show that theory is not merely an end in itself but an adjunct to the understanding and playing of music.

1. Study the extract from the Sonatina in G minor (1780) by Benda, printed opposite, $\boxed{25}$
    then answer the questions below.

(a) Describe fully the melodic intervals numbered $\boxed{1}$ and $\boxed{2}$ in bars 4 and 8.

    1 (bar 4) ....

    2 (bar 8) .... (4)

(b) Write out the right-hand part of bars 15–16 as you think it should be played.

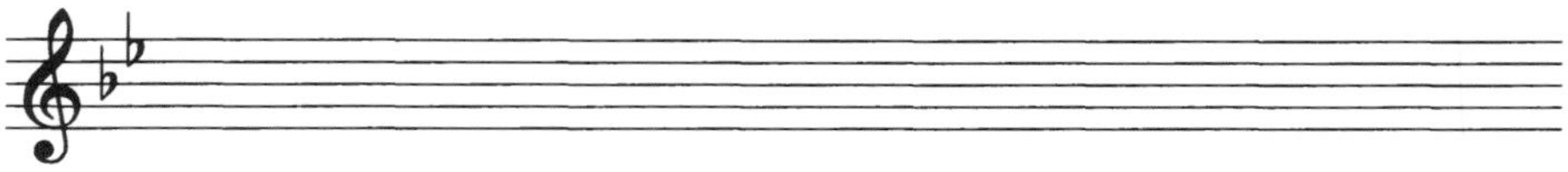

    (3)

(c) Identify the chords marked * in bars 3 and 13 by writing on the dotted lines below. Use either
    words or symbols. State the position of each chord, whether it is major, minor, augmented or
    diminished and the prevailing key.

    bar 3 .... key ....

    bar 13 .... key .... (8)

(d) Mark clearly on the score, using the appropriate capital letter for identification, ONE example of
    each of the following:

    A an imperfect cadence in the tonic key

    B a lower auxiliary note (4)

(e) Show the main phrase structure of the extract by drawing square brackets ($\boxed{}$)
    above each of the phrases, as shown above the first phrase. (3)

(f) Name the key in:

    (i) bars 9–10 ....

    (ii) bars 11–12 ....

    (iii) bars 15–16 .... (3)

2.   Study the final part of an Étude for piano printed opposite and then answer the questions below.

(a)   Mark clearly on the score, using the appropriate capital letter for identification, one example of each of the following **in the first eight bars**:

    A   a dominant 7th chord in first inversion in F♯ minor
    B   an inverted (inner) pedal lasting three bars (mark ⌊_____ **B** _____⌋)
    C   melodic imitation of one bar, an octave higher than the initial statement
            (mark ⌈_____ **C** _____⌉)
    D   a ⁶₄ (ic) chord on the dominant note of C♯ minor

    in the last four bars:

    E   a dominant 7th in root position in C♯ minor

(b)   Write out in full the left-hand part in bar 3 as you think it should be played.

(c)   Complete the following statements:

    (i)   The extract shows many examples of melodic decoration. In bar 1 the left-hand D♯ is an

            .... and the C𝗑 in bar 6 is a ....

            The left-hand final C♯ of bar 10 is a(n) .... and there is a

            later example of this in the right-hand final note of bar ....

    (ii) The harmonic and melodic procedure in bars 11 and 12 is known as ....

    (iii) At the start the composer marks the piece **Lento**, meaning ...., and

            sempre tenuto, meaning ....

(d)   The left-hand melody could very effectively be played on the cello. Write out the first phrase (from bar 1 to the second beat of bar 4) at the same pitch, but in the tenor clef:

(e)   Describe fully each of the melodic intervals marked ⌊___⌋ in the left-hand part:

    1 (bar 4)   ....
    2 (bar 10)   ....
    3 (bar 12)   ....

(f)   Underline ONE composer from the following list who you think is the writer of this piece.

            Haydn   Chopin   Debussy   Schoenberg

    Give THREE reasons for your choice:

    1.   ....
    2.   ....
    3.   ....

3.   Study the extract from a Minuet for keyboard printed opposite and then answer the questions below.

(a) Mark clearly on the score, using the appropriate capital letter for identification, one example of each of the following **in bars 1–16**:

    A   the top five notes of an ascending melodic minor scale used in a descending pattern in the right hand (mark ⌐   **A**   ⌐)

    B   an inverted tonic pedal (mark ⌐   **B**   ⌐)

    C   modulation to F major (mark ⌐   **C**   ⌐)

    D   a melodic sequence a tone lower than the previous two bars (mark ⌐   **D**   ⌐)

(b) Give the names of the notes of melodic decoration marked * in bars 4, 5 and 15.

    bar 4   ....

    bar 5   ....

    bar 15   ....

(c) Draw a circle round a note which is not essential to the harmony in bar 23.

    What kind of melodic decoration note is this? ....

(d) Show the phrase structure of the extract by drawing square brackets (⌐   ⌐) over each of the main phrases.

(e) Bars 1–8 and 9–16 are clearly related. Point out three *differences* between them.

    1. ....

    2. ....

    3. ....

(f) Identify the chords numbered **1**, **2** and **3**. Use either words or symbols. State the position of each chord, whether it is major, minor, augmented or diminished and the prevailing key.

    1 (bar 10) .... key ....

    2 (bar 21) .... key ....

    3 (bar 23) .... key ....

(g) Complete the following statements:

    (i)   The texture is made up of .... parts.

    (ii) From bar 17 there is .... between the left-hand parts, using a motif first heard in bar ....

    (iii) The key of the piece is ...., but in bars 19–20 the key is ....

    (iv) The **absence** of dynamics, of marks for a sustaining pedal and the **use** of ornaments and contra-puntal style suggest that the music comes from the .... period. A likely instrument for which the piece was composed is the .... and a likely composer is ...., who included many Minuets in his suites and partitas.

4.   Study the opening of the third movement of Beethoven's String Quartet Op. 135, printed opposite, and then answer the questions below.

(a)   Give the meaning of:

Lento assai   ....

cantante e tranquillo   ....

sotto voce (bar 3)   ....

♩ ♪ (bar 7, first violin)   ....

(b)   What is the key in:

bars 1–6?   ....

bar 7?   ....

bar 8?   ....

(c)   Mark clearly on the score, using the appropriate capital letter for identification, one example of each of the following **in bars 1–9**:

A   a dominant 7th chord in second inversion in D♭ major
B   a dominant 7th chord in root position in B♭ minor
C   a note which can only be played on an open string
D   three bars that form a melodic sequence
E   a perfect 4th played as a double stop

and from bar 8 onwards:

F   a subdominant chord in first inversion
G   successive tonic chords in root position, first inversion and second inversion
      (mark ⌐_____G_____⌐)

(d)   Describe fully the intervals formed from:

(i)   the lowest and highest notes played by the cello   ....

(ii)   the lowest and highest notes played by the 1st violin   ....

(e)   Complete the following statements:

(i)   The pitches of the non-harmony notes played by the 1st violin in bar 5 are ....
       and the name given to these notes of melodic decoration is ....

(ii)   The only instrument not required to play a double stop is the ....

(iii) The instrument with the most limited pitch range used here is the ...., with
       its notes all within the interval of a ....

(iv)   The motif played by the 1st violin in bar 10 is played in the same bar by the cello in ....
       form and in bar 11 it appears again, played by the .... an ....
       lower than the initial statement by the 1st violin. Another appearance is in bar .... where it is
       played by the ...., this time an .... higher than bar 10.

5.   Study the extract from a Minuet for keyboard printed opposite and then answer the questions below.

(a) Mark clearly on the score, using the appropriate capital letter for identification, one example of each of the following:

In the first section (up to bar 10):

A   a melodic interval of a rising major 10th (compound major 3rd) in the right-hand part

B   a $^6_4$–$^5_3$ (Ic–V) progression in the dominant key

In the second section (bar 10 onwards):

C   a two-bar melodic sequence a 7th higher than the previous two bars (mark ⌐   C   ⌐)

D   a harmonic interval of an augmented 4th in the bass clef

E   three bars in which the bass rises chromatically (mark ⌐   E   ⌐)

(b) Write out the right-hand part of bar 4 as you think it should be played.

(c) (i)   What term is used for the notes of melodic decoration marked **1** and **2** in bar 15?

       1 ....   **2** ....

     (ii) In the same bar, label clearly with **1** and **2**, two further notes which have the same name and function.

(d) Show the main phrase structure of the right-hand melody (mark ⌐   ⌐ above each phrase).

(e) Complete the following statements:

     (i)   The Minuet begins in the key of .... A modulation to the key of .... is made in bars 5–6 but only confirmed with a .... cadence in this key in bars 9–10. The key in bars 11–12 is .... and in bars 13–14 it is ....

     (ii) The melodic interval between the second and third right-hand notes of bar 17 is a .... and the chord on the second quaver of bar 21 is .... in the tonic key.

     (iii) The sign used above the right-hand F♯s in bar 6 is called a .... and normally means ....

(f) Underline the name of **ONE** composer who you think is likely to have written this Minuet.

            Ravel   Corelli   Haydn   Bartók   Couperin   J. S. Bach

     Give **THREE** reasons for your choice:

     1.   ....
     2.   ....
     3.   ....

6.   Study the extract from the first of Finzi's Five Bagatelles for clarinet and piano, printed opposite, and then answer the questions below.

(a)   Identify the chords marked * in bars 1, 3, 5, 6 and 8 of the **piano part** by writing on the dotted lines below. Use either words or symbols. State the position of each chord and whether it is major, minor, augmented or diminished. Treat them all as in the key of E major.

bar 1 ....

bar 3 ....

bar 5 ....

bar 6 ....

bar 8 ....

(b)   What term is used for each of the numbered notes of melodic decoration in the piano part of bars 2, 8 and 15?

1 (bar 2) ....

2 (bar 8) ....

3 (bar 15) ....

(c)   Give the meaning of:

(i)   **Poco meno mosso**   ....

(ii)   *semplice*   ....

(iii)   – (e.g. clarinet, bar 15, beat 1)   ....

(d)   Answer TRUE or UNTRUE to each of the following statements:

(i)   In bar 11 the clarinet plays the same melody as the piano played in bar 1, but now sounding at a different pitch.   ....

(ii)   All the notes (both hands) in the piano part of bars 19–20 can be found in one or other form of the B♭ minor scale.   ....

(iii)   The interval between the highest and lowest written notes played by the clarinet in bars 11 to the end of this extract is a compound perfect 4th.   ....

(e)   Write out at concert pitch the clarinet part of bars 15–16. Use the appropriate key signature.

(f)   (i)   Give the bar numbers of two later appearances in the clarinet part of the piano right-hand theme in bar 1.   Bar .... and bar ....

(ii)   In the piano part of the bars you have specified, name two *differences* from the piano part in bar 1, and one similarity.

Differences   1.   ....

2.   ....

Similarity   1.   ....

(g)   Name the procedure taking place between bars 18–19 of the piano part, top line.   ....

Question 5

As with Question 4, this tests your understanding of a given extract of music, the main difference being that Question 5 is more likely to include a full score for an orchestra or a larger ensemble, or a vocal score with accompaniment. **Occasionally, one slightly longer extract with questions worth a total of 50 marks may be used to cover the ground included in Questions 4 and 5.**

The score will not normally have more than nine staves sounding simultaneously in a system. Instruments will usually be restricted to those used in the standard orchestra, that is the piccolo, flute, oboe, clarinet, bassoon, horn, trumpet, trombone, tuba, timpani, bass drum, side drum, cymbals, triangle and strings. Transposing instruments will normally be limited to those in B♭, A or F. Instrument names will be given in English, French, German or Italian and will be stated in full at the beginning of the extract or, when appropriate, at the beginning of a new system where they are first used. Sometimes you may be asked to identify them.

Vocal scores may also be used, including solo voices and/or SATB chorus (sometimes with divided parts) but the total number of simultaneously sounding staves will not usually exceed nine. This will include any necessary orchestral accompaniment which will be reduced to piano score.

Many of the questions asked in Question 4 could also be asked here: for example, there might be questions on keys, notes of melodic decoration, ornaments, particular chords, terms and symbols, intervals and so on, but in any one exam paper, Questions 4 and 5 will normally complement each other without testing too much of the same ground.

Question 5 will, in particular, test your grasp of the score: for example, the way it is laid out, the various instrumental families, the various clefs they use, transposing instruments and others which do not sound at the written pitch, those that have a single reed, a double reed, and so on.

There may be questions testing a more detailed understanding of the score: for example, the various articulations and the meanings of signs and terms; of I, II, a2, div, unis, up and down bows, open strings, pizz., arco, sul ponticello, sul G, con sordini; the standard abbreviations for repeated figures, and a general grasp of the effective range and capabilities of the instruments. You may be asked more general questions, for example, on how a mood or climax is achieved, or on the effect of string, wind or choral writing.

Almost invariably you will be asked to write out, at concert pitch, a few bars of one or more of the parts for transposing instruments. Remember that a horn in F sounds a perfect 5th lower than written, the clarinet in B♭ and the trumpet in B♭ sound a tone lower than written, and the clarinet in A sounds a minor third lower. Also remember that the double bass is written in C but sounds an octave lower than written, while the piccolo sounds an octave higher than its written notes.

The extracts, which are usually much shorter in length than those for Question 4, may come from the Baroque period through to the present day but will not normally exceed the specifications given earlier. Questions on phrase structure are much less likely because of the shorter extracts, but you may be asked about the use of a motif or theme among different sections and instruments.

Much useful information about orchestral instruments is given in *The AB Guide to Music Theory*, Part II, Chapters 19–22.

Question 5   Sample Questions

Here are a number of exam-style practice tests. As in the practice tests for Question 4, the first extract shows the typical number of questions that would be asked in an exam, together with an example of how the marks might be distributed, adding up to the usual total of 25 for the whole exercise. Tests 2 to 6 contain more questions than you would be asked in an exam. Again, as for Question 4, marks for individual sections or questions can vary from paper to paper according to difficulty and time likely to be spent on them.

The questions asked are representative of the kinds of wording used and the typical requirements of exam papers.

Finally, there could be no better preparation than an intensive study of short extracts of music, first with the score, then while listening to repeated performances. In this way the visual impression develops the aural senses and the ear confirms what the eye has seen.

1.   Study the extract from an orchestral piece printed opposite and then answer the questions below.   [25]

(a) Which instrument in the extract:

(i)   plays in unison with the 2nd violin throughout?   ....

(ii)   is the only one which *has to* use an open string?   ....

(iii) sounds an octave lower than it is written?   ....   (6)

(b) Write out the parts for solo clarinet and solo horn in bars 4–5 as they would sound at concert pitch. Use the appropriate clef and key signature for each.

Clarinet

Horn   (4)

(c) Mark clearly on the score, using the appropriate capital letter for identification, one example of each of the following.

A   a melodic sequence lasting three bars (mark [A   ]).

B   four bars where clarinet and horn sound an octave apart (mark [B   ]).

C   a place where an instrument is to be plucked lightly.   (6)

(d) Complete the following statements:

The instrument marked to play the most quietly in the extract is the ....

in bar .... The loudest bar in the extract will be bar .... for the following three reasons:

1.   ....

2.   ....

3.   ....   (5)

(e) Underline ONE period from those printed below during which you think the piece might have been written:

1650–1725   1725–1800   1800–1870   1870–1925

Give three reasons for your answer:

1.   ....

2.   ....

3.   ....   (4)

2.   Study the extract printed opposite and then answer the questions below.

(a) Mark clearly on the score, using the appropriate capital letter for identification, one example of each of the following:

    (i)   **in bars 9–12** (the figures have been omitted from the bass in these bars):

        A   a place where the viola plays the highest sounding note, with other instruments

        B   a dominant 7th chord in third inversion (V^7d) without a third

        C   a $^6_4$–$^5_3$ (Ic–V) progression at an imperfect cadence

    (ii) **from anywhere in the extract**:

        D   a note of anticipation in the flute part

        E   an inverted dominant pedal (mark ⌐   **E**   ¬)

        F   a harmonic/melodic sequence (mark ⌐   **F**   ¬)

        G   a lower auxiliary note in the flute part

(b) Complete the following statements:

    (i)   **Largo** means ....

    (ii) In bars 3–4 there is a modulation to the key of ....

    (iii) The phrase lengths are four bars, four bars, ... bars and .... bars.

    (iv) The keyboard instrument most likely to have harmonised the figured bass is a ....

    (v)   Two differences between bars 13–14 and 15–16 are:

        1.   ....

        2.   ....

(c) Write out the flute part for bars 12 and 19 as you think it should be played.

Bar 12   Bar 19

(d) Answer **TRUE** or **UNTRUE** to each of the following statements:

The flute and violin I parts are identical. ....

Apart from the modulation in bars 3–4 the piece is entirely in A major. ....

In bar 17 there is imitation between violin II and bass. ....

There is no supertonic chord with 7th in the extract. ....

The D in bar 18 of the flute part is an unaccented passing note. ....

(e) In addition to a keyboard instrument, which other instruments might also have played the part marked 'Bass'?

Woodwind ....   Strings ....

(f) Underline **ONE** period during which you think this piece was composed:

          1600–1675   1675–1800   1800–1900

Give three reasons for your choice:

    1.   ....

    2.   ....

    3.   ....

3.　Study the extract from Kodály's *Te Deum* for soprano and tenor soloists, SATB chorus and orchestra (here reduced for piano) printed opposite and then answer the questions below.

(a)　(i)　Identify the chords marked * in bars 3 and 10 by writing on the dotted lines below. Use either words or symbols. State the position of each chord, whether it is major, minor, augmented or diminished, and the prevailing key.

bar 3　..　key　...........................

bar 10　...　key　...........................

(ii)　What do all but one of the chords in the **chorus part** have in common? ....

....

(b)　Compare bars 2–4 and 9–11 then name one **similarity** and three **differences** between them.

Similarity　1.　...

Differences　1.　...

2.　...

3.　...

(c)　The chords sounding in bars 2–4 of the piano reduction are played in the orchestra by two clarinets in A (right hand) and two horns in F (left hand). Write out the parts as they would appear for the players (do not use key signatures).

Clarinets

Horns

(d)　Mark clearly on the score, using the appropriate capital letter for identification, one example of each of the following:

A　a place in the chorus part where the chord is minor
B　an accented passing note (or appoggiatura) in the solo soprano part
C　a complete phrase with notes in canon, between the two solo voices (mark ⌐　　　C　　　⌐)

(e)　Complete the following statements:

(i)　The composer achieves rhythmic interest and continuity in the vocal writing by the overlapping of the .... and .... parts.

(ii)　The most animated rhythmic movement in the extract is in bars .... of the .... part.

(iii)　'Homophonic' means .... as shown by the .... parts. 'Polyphonic' means .... as shown by the .... parts.

4.   Study the extract from Hindemith's Concerto for Orchestra printed opposite and then answer the questions below.

(a)   Mark clearly on the score, using the appropriate capital letter for identification, one example of each of the named melodic intervals:

(i)   in bars 1–8:

A   a falling major 7th in a wind part
B   a falling diminished 5th in a string part

(ii)   in bars 9–12:

C   a falling chromatic semitone in a wind part
D   a rising minor 7th in a string part

(b)   Complete the following statements:

(i)   In bar 1, **im gleichen Zeitmaß** means 'at the same speed'. **Immer** means ....

'**Sehr schnell**' means ....

(ii)   *veloce* means ....

(iii)   The only exact doubling of a theme at the unison is between the .... and

.... in bars .... to ....

(iv)   The word 'arco' in the cello part in bar 6 means .... and implies

that the last time the cello played, it played ....

(v)   The theme played by the oboe in bars 11–12 has already been played by the ....

in bars .... to .... and bars .... to ....

(c)   Write out the clarinet part as it would sound at concert pitch in bars 4–6. Do not use a key signature.

(d)   Answer **TRUE** or **UNTRUE** to each of the following statements:

(i)   The rhythmic grouping of notes is regular throughout.   ....

(ii)   All the notes of the Violin I part in bars 1–5 can be found in the two forms of the B♭ minor scale.

....

(iii)   The clarinet is the only instrument used here which does not sound at the written pitch.

....

(iv)   The extract is homophonic rather than contrapuntal.   ....

(e)   Name three features of the extract which would suggest that it is from the twentieth and not the nineteenth century.

1.   ....

2.   ....

3.   ....

Immer im gleichen Zeitmaß, jedoch nicht eilen (Sehr schnell)

5.   Study the extract from Mozart's *A Musical Joke* K522, printed opposite, and then answer the questions below.

(a) Mark clearly on the score, using the appropriate capital letter for identification, one example of each of the following **in the last eight bars**:

   A   a note which can only be played on an open string
   B   a dominant 7th chord in root position in the tonic key
   C   a bar which has the successive harmonic intervals of a perfect octave, perfect 5th and major 3rd between the same instruments

(b) Complete the following statements:

   (i)   The extract starts in the key of .... In bars 7–8 it modulates to the key of .... After the double bar, further modulations take place, to the key of .... in bar 19 and to the key of .... in bar 26, before returning to the key of .... in bar 28.

   (ii) There is a rising sequence in the melody and harmony between bars .... and ....

(c) Identify the chords marked * in bars 3 and 25. Use either words or symbols. State the position of each chord, whether it is major, minor, augmented or diminished, and the prevailing key.

   bar 3   ....   key ....
   bar 25 .... and .... key ....

(d) Name three features of the extract which contribute to the intended playfulness of this *Musical Joke*.
   1.   ....
   2.   ....
   3.   ....

(e) Answer **TRUE** or **UNTRUE** to each of the following statements:

   (i)   The phrase lengths are regular, mainly four bars but with some of two bars.   ....

   (ii) The interval between the 1st and 2nd violins is a third throughout.   ....

   (iii) The biggest leap in the viola part is the interval of a minor 10th (compound minor 3rd).
         ....

   (iv) The bottom part (Basso) would not include cellos.   ....

(f) Write out in full, as they would sound at concert pitch, the parts for horns in bars 15–18. Use the appropriate clef and key signature.

6.   Study the extract from the second movement of Mendelssohn's Piano Concerto No. 2 in D minor, Op. 40, printed opposite, and then answer the questions below.

(a) Give the meaning of:

Adagio   ....

Molto sostenuto   ....

(b) Complete the following statements:

The extract opens in the key of .... and the first phrase ends with an imperfect cadence

in bars .... The second phrase passes through G minor to the key of ....

with a perfect cadence in bars .... A new melodic phrase lasting .... bars modulates

to the key of .... in bars 9–10 and, when repeated, modulates back to ....

The next theme, starting in bar 12, lasts for .... bars and is similar to the main theme in that the

first .... notes are the same. The phrase is repeated with the 1st violins doubled by the ....

....

(c) Write out bars 16–18 of the parts for clarinets as they would sound at concert pitch. Use the appropriate clef and key signature.

(d) Mark clearly on the score, using the appropriate capital letter for identification, one example of each of the following:

A   the lowest sounding note in bar 7, second crotchet beat
B   a note which can only be played on an open string in bars 1–12
C   a rising interval of an augmented 4th in a string part in bars 1–8
D   a falling interval of a diminished 4th in a string part in bars 1–8
E   a theme played at the interval of an octave by woodwind instruments
F   a note of anticipation in the first violin part in bars 1–8

(e) Identify the chords marked * above the string parts in bars 1, 2, 10 and 15. Use either words or symbols. State the position of each chord, whether it is major, minor, augmented or diminished, and the prevailing key.

bar 1   ....   key ....

bar 2   ....   key ....

bar 10   ....   key ....

bar 15   ....   key ....

(f) Name four reasons you would give to convince someone that this piece was **not** written in the Baroque period.

1. ....

2. ....

3. ....

4. ....

Answers to Question 4

These are specimen answers. Alternative responses are often possible, and will receive credit if they accurately answer part of or the full requirements of the question.

1. **(a)** **1** diminished 3rd   **2** minor 10th [compound minor 3rd]

   (b)  *(other versions possible)*

   (c) bar 3: ii°^{7}b (diminished); G minor   bar 13: V^{7}b (major); B♭ major

   (d) **A** bar 4, beat 1   **B** bar 7, right hand, last G

   (e) *(other versions possible):*

   (f) **(i)** B♭ major   **(ii)** F major   **(iii)** B♭ major

2. **(a)** **A** bar 4, last semiquaver   **B** bars 5–7 (C♯)
        C bar 2 (right hand)   **D** bar 7, beat 2 *or* bar 8, beat 2
        E bar 13, last semiquaver (*or* bar 14, last quaver)

   (b)  *or*

   (c) **(i)** accented passing note [appoggiatura];
            lower (chromatic) auxiliary note; note of anticipation; (bar) 12

        (ii) sequence
        (iii) slow; always sustained [held]

   (d)

   (e) **1** minor 10th [compound minor 3rd]
        2 diminished 7th   **3** diminished 5th

   (f) Chopin (Study in C♯ minor, Op. 25 No. 7)
   wrote many études for piano; expressive markings; rich harmony; embellished cantabile line

3. **(a)** **A** bar 7 (R.H.)   **B** bars 5–6 (R.H.)
        C bars 3–4 *or* 11–12   **D** bars 11–12

   (b) bar 4:   accented passing note [appoggiatura]
        bar 5:   lower auxiliary note   bar 15:   changing note [échappée]

   (c) first F; unaccented passing note

   (d) regular 4-bar phrasing *or* 4+4+8 :‖ 4+4

   (e) more flowing bass part in bars 9–14; suspensions in lower R.H. part
   from bar 9; bar 11 shows altered melody

(f) **1**   ii⁷ (minor); F major (iv⁷ (minor); D minor is also acceptable)
  2   (♯)vii°c (diminished); D minor   **3**   V⁷ (major); D minor

(g) **(i)**   3   **(ii)**   imitation; (bar) 1   **(iii)**   D minor; G minor
  (iv)   Baroque; harpsichord; J. S. Bach
    (French Suite in D minor, BWV 812)

4. (a)   very slow;   in a singing style and calm;   in an undertone;
    slightly detached but in the same bow stroke, heavy, with pressure

(b)   D♭ major;   B♭ minor;   E♭ minor

(c)   **A**   bar 3, beat 2   **B**   bar 7, beat 1
  C   viola C, bar 6 *or* bar 7; *or* cello C, bar 4 *or* bar 9
  D   bars 7–9   **E**   cello, second beat of bar 3 (*or* 5)
  F   bar 11, last quaver   **G**   bar 9, beat 2 – bar 10

(d)   **(i)**   compound perfect 4th   **(ii)**   compound major 6th

(e)   **(i)**   C (first) and B♭;   unaccented passing notes
  (ii)   viola   **(iii)**   viola;   diminished 5th
  (iv)   inverted;   cello;   octave;   (bar) 12;   1st violin;   octave

5. (a)   **A**   bar 5, notes 2–3   **B**   bar 9, beats 2 and 3
  C   bar 12, beat 3 – bar 14, first note
  D   bar 19, beat 3   **E**   bars 14–16

(b)   *Other versions possible (such as the second, for a faster tempo):*

(c)   **(i)**   **1**   accented passing note [appoggiatura]
      2   chromatic lower auxiliary note
  (ii)   **1** on F♯, 5th semiquaver (*or* D♯, 9th semiquaver)
      2 on B♯, 11th semiquaver

(d)   2+2+6 :‖: 2+4+6 :‖   (all phrases start on 3rd beat of the bar)

(e)   **(i)**   B major;   F♯ major;   perfect;   C♯ minor;   B major
  (ii)   compound minor 7th; iib   **(iii)**   wedge; a very short staccato

(f)   Haydn (Sonata in B minor, No. 32)
    texture comprises melody with chordal accompaniment;
    balanced (periodic) phrasing; simple, functional harmonies;
    ornamentation; use of triadic, scalic and turn-like figures;
    Haydn wrote many Minuets

6. (a)   V⁷c (major);   V⁷d (major);   ii⁷ (minor);   iiib (minor);   ii⁷b (minor)

(b)   **1** lower auxiliary note   **2** unaccented passing note   **3** appoggiatura

(c)   **(i)**   a little less speed (movement) *or* a bit slower
  (ii)   simple *or* simply *or* plain
  (iii)   hold for full value – emphasise *or* sustain, with pressure

(d)   **(i)**   UNTRUE   **(ii)**   TRUE   **(iii)**   UNTRUE

(e)

(f)   (Bar) 11 and (bar) 19.
    Differences: piano part doesn't incorporate melody
          piano an octave lower in bar 11
          piano above melody in bar 19, and scalic
    Similarity: piano bass rises by step

(g)   Enharmonic change

Answers to Question 5

These are specimen answers. Alternative responses are often possible, and will receive credit if they accurately answer part of or the full requirements of the question.

1. (a) (i) 2nd flute   **(ii)** viola   **(iii)** double bass

(b)

Clarinet

Horn

(c) **A** bars 9–11   **B** bars 6–9   **C** bar 9, cello

(d) 1st clarinet; (bar) 1; (bar) 12
1. tutti (everyone playing)
2. highest notes in the extract for most instruments
3. *sf* marking *or* climax of *cresc.* from bar 10

(e) 1800–1870 (Berlioz – *Symphonie Fantastique*)
horn and clarinet solos; some chromaticism; double bass divisi; wide dynamic range; detailed playing instructions; comparatively simple harmonies and phrasing do not suggest a later date

2. (a) **A** bar 10, second note   **B** bar 10, last quaver   **C** bar 12
D bar 19, last note   **E** bar 9 – bar 11, beat 1
F bar 4, beat 3 to bar 6, beat 1 (*or* bar 7, beat 1)
G G♯ in bar 3 *or* C♯ in bar 7

(b) (i) slow *or* stately *or* broad   **(ii)** E major
(iii) four (bars); eight (bars)   **(iv)** harpsichord
(v) 1. 2nd violin and bass interchange their notes in quavers (bar 15)
2. extra note in 2nd violin in bar 16

(c)

Bar 12   *(other versions possible)*   Bar 19   *(other versions possible)*

(d) TRUE;   TRUE;   TRUE;   UNTRUE;   UNTRUE

(e) bassoon; cello [lute, etc., also possible]

(f) 1675–1800 (Arne – Dance from *Comus*)
figured bass; stately dance style; ornaments at cadence points; simple, diatonic harmony with limited modulation; use of sequence; some use of contrapuntal texture and imitation

3. (a) (i) bar 3: V^7 (major); F♯ minor   bar 10: V^7 (major); B minor
(ii) all in root position

(b) Similarity: same chord progression
Differences: bars 9–11 are a perfect 4th higher; they use *crescendo*; different orchestration; differences in layout of tenor and bass parts (extra notes/divided parts/rest in bass)

(c)

Clarinets

pp

Horns

(bass clef equally acceptable for horns)

    (d) **A**   bar 4, beats 1–3 (*or* bar 11, beats 1–3)

          B   bar 3, beat 4 *or* bar 7, beat 4 *or* bar 10, beat 4   **C** bars 6–8

    (e) **(i)** solo; chorus   **(ii)** 6–7; orchestra

          (iii) chordal [parts moving together in same rhythm]; chorus; simultaneous melodic lines moving independently; solo

4. **(a)** **A**   flute, bar 3, beat 4 – bar 4, beat 1

          B   violin I, bar 5, 5th–6th quavers

          C   oboe, bar 11, beat 4 – bar 12, beat 1

          D   cello, bar 9, beats 2–4 *or* violin/viola, bar 12, beat 1

    (b) **(i)** always; very fast   **(ii)** swiftly

          (iii) bassoon (I) (and) cello; (bars) 6 (to) 11

          (iv) bowed; pizzicato *or* plucked

          (v) flute; (bars) 1 (to) 2; (bars) 7 (to) 8

    (c)

    (d) **(i)** UNTRUE   **(ii)** TRUE   **(iii)** UNTRUE   **(iv)** UNTRUE

    (e) dissonant; lack of tonal harmony; polytonality; no key signature but many accidentals; parts shift between unrelated keys

5. **(a)** **A**   viola, bar 25, beat 2   **B** bar 27, last quaver

          C   horns, bar 27

    (b) **(i)** F major; D minor; A♭ major; F minor; F major

          (ii) (bars) 10 (and) 18

    (c) bar 3:   iib (minor chord); F major

          bar 25: ic (minor chord) and V (major chord); F minor

    (d) very short phrases; short notes; sudden dynamic contrasts; unexpected modulations; lively pace; simple ideas; repetitive rhythm; changes from major to minor (e.g. last 5 bars)

    (e) **(i)** TRUE   **(ii)** UNTRUE   **(iii)** TRUE   **(iv)** UNTRUE

    (f)

6. **(a)** slow; very sustained

    (b) B♭ major;   (bars) 3–4;   F major;   (bars) 7–8;   2 (bars);

          C minor;   B♭ major;   4 (bars);   3 (notes);   1st flute

    (c)

    (d) **A**   C in the double basses   **B**   viola C, bar 11, beat 1

          C   2nd violin, bar 3   **D**   2nd violin, bar 6, beat 2

          E   clarinet and bassoon, bars 8–10   **F**   bar 7, final semiquaver A

    (e) bar 1   V^7 (major chord); B♭ major

          bar 2   V^{7}d (major chord); B♭ major

          bar 10   iv (minor chord); C minor

          bar 15   Ic (major chord); B♭ major

    (f) use of clarinets; no figured bass; frequent use of slurs; large number of dynamic and articulation markings; cadences at regular intervals; functional harmonies with some chromaticism; piano concerto not a standard medium; melody-dominated style with mainly thick-textured accompaniment